Delaware

By Kelly Bennett

Consultants
Nanci R. Vargus, Ed.D.
Assistant Professor of Literacy
University of Indianapolis
Indianapolis, Indiana

Jennifer L. Minchini
Red Clay Consolidated School District
Wilmington, Delaware

Children's Press®
A Division of Scholastic Inc.
New York   Toronto   London   Auckland   Sydney
Mexico City   New Delhi   Hong Kong
Danbury, Connecticut

Designer: Herman Adler Design
Photo Researcher: Caroline Anderson
The photo on the cover shows the Old State House in Dover, Delaware.

Library of Congress Cataloging-in-Publication Data

Bennett, Kelly.
  Delaware / by Kelly Bennett ; consultant, Nanci R. Vargus.
    p. cm. — (Rookie read-about geography)
  Includes index.
  ISBN 0-516-22752-1 (lib. bdg.)   0-516-25156-2 (pbk.)
  1. Delaware—Juvenile literature. 2. Delaware—Geography—Juvenile
literature. I. Vargus, Nanci Reginelli. II. Title. III. Series.
  F164.3.B46 2004
  975.1'044—dc22
                                          2004000468

CHILDREN'S PRESS, and ROOKIE READ-ABOUT®,
and associated logos are trademarks and or registered trademarks
of Scholastic Library Publishing. SCHOLASTIC and associated logos
are trademarks and or registered trademarks of Scholastic Inc.

1 2 3 4 5 6 7 8 9 10 R 13 12 11 10 09 08 07 06 05 04

The ladybug is the state bug for which state?

Delaware!

Can you find Delaware
on this map?

Delaware borders
Pennsylvania, Maryland,
and the Atlantic Ocean.

CANADA

WASHINGTON
OREGON
IDAHO
MONTANA
NORTH DAKOTA
MINNESOTA
NEW HAMPSHIRE
VERMONT
MAINE
MICHIGAN
WYOMING
SOUTH DAKOTA
WISCONSIN
MASSACHUSETTS
NEW YORK
RHODE ISLAND
CONNECTICUT
NEW JERSEY
NEVADA
UTAH
NEBRASKA
IOWA
OHIO
PENNSYLVANIA
DELAWARE
CALIFORNIA
COLORADO
KANSAS
ILLINOIS
INDIANA
WEST VIRGINIA
MARYLAND
Washington, D.C.
MISSOURI
KENTUCKY
VIRGINIA
ARIZONA
NEW MEXICO
OKLAHOMA
ARKANSAS
TENNESSEE
NORTH CAROLINA
TEXAS
MISSISSIPPI
ALABAMA
GEORGIA
SOUTH CAROLINA
LOUISIANA
FLORIDA

ALASKA
CANADA
MEXICO
HAWAII

North
West
East
South

5

Bald cypress trees in Trap Pond State Park

There are forests, farms, wetlands, and beaches in Delaware.

Most of the land is low and flat.

Pumpkin farm

The highest part of
Delaware is in the north.
Forests cover much of
this hilly area.

Wilmington is Delaware's
largest city. It has many
factories. They make cars,
paper, chemicals, and clothing.

Banks and credit card companies have offices here, too.

Wilmington

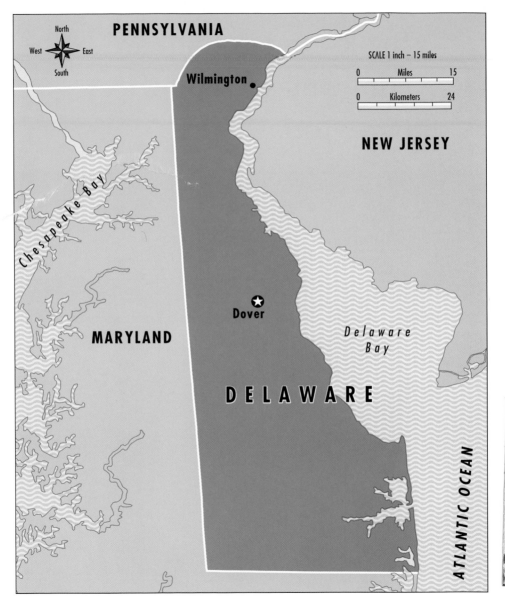

Dover is the state capital. It is located in the center of the state.

Dover is in the center
of farmlands, too.

Farmers grow corn,
wheat, soybeans, and holly.
Holly is used to make
Christmas wreaths.

Holly

16

Many farmers in Delaware raise chickens. The state bird is the blue hen chicken.

Do you see its blue feathers?

Delaware has about 50 lakes and many streams and rivers.

The most important river is the Delaware River. Ships carry goods down this river to Delaware Bay.

19

Much of the coast of
Delaware Bay is wetlands.
This land is under water
most of the time.

Young fish, turtles, and reptiles hide in the marsh grasses. Shore birds find food here.

Great Blue Heron

Fishing is an important job in this area.

Some people gather clams, oysters, and crabs. Steamed crab makes a tasty meal!

This man has a crab in his hands.

Delaware's beaches are in the south. People come to play in the sand and water.

The boardwalk at
Rehoboth Beach has
fun games and rides.

Birds visit Delaware, too.
They stop to rest and eat
as they fly north or south.

Bird-watchers come to
see them!

Which part of Delaware
do you like best?

Words You Know

beach

blue hen chicken

crab

factory

30

forest

holly

wetlands

Wilmington

31

Index

About the Author

Kelly Bennett visited Delaware when she was a young girl. She loved eating crab on the beach! Kelly enjoys traveling with her family and writing about places she visits. She lives in Katy, Texas.

Photo Credits

Photographs © 2004: Corbis Images: 19, 24, 30 top left (Kevin Fleming), 6 (David Muench); David J. Forbert: 7, 23, 30 bottom left; Delaware Tourism Office: 16, 30 top right; ImageState/Tony Sweet: 9, 31 top left; Kevin Fleming: 10, 28, 30 bottom right; Photo Researchers, NY: 20, 31 bottom left (Michael P. Gadomski), 27 (Jeff Lepore), 11, 31 bottom right (Joe Sohm), 21 (Vanessa Vick); Robertstock.com/G. Ahrens: 15, 31 top right; Superstock, Inc./David Forbert: cover; TRIP Photo Library/Jeff Greenberg: 25; Unicorn Stock Photos/Richard Baker: 3.

Maps by Bob Italiano